LOST IN THE MOUNTAINS

BY CORINN CODYE

Reading Skills for Life

Level B

Book 1

AGS®
American Guidance Service, Inc.
Circle Pines, Minnesota 55014-1796
1-800-328-2560

Development and editorial services provided by Straight Line Editorial Development, Inc.

Illustrations: Wendy Cantor

© 2002 AGS® American Guidance Service, Inc., Circle Pines, MN 55014-1796. All rights reserved, including translation. No part of this publication may be reproduced or transmitted in any form or by any means without written permission from the publisher.

Printed in the United States of America

ISBN 0-7854-2652-3

Product Number 91713

A 0 9 8 7 6 5 4 3 2

Contents

Chapter 1 Family Bonding 5

Chapter 2 Madman on the Road . 10

Chapter 3 The Long Night 17

Chapter 4 Our Plan 24

Chapter 5 Ben and Fred 30

Chapter 6 The Streambed 33

Chapter 7 Snake! 39

Chapter 8 The Car Phone 44

Chapter 9 Get Out of the Way! ... 52

Chapter 10 Ghost Ranch Outpost ..57

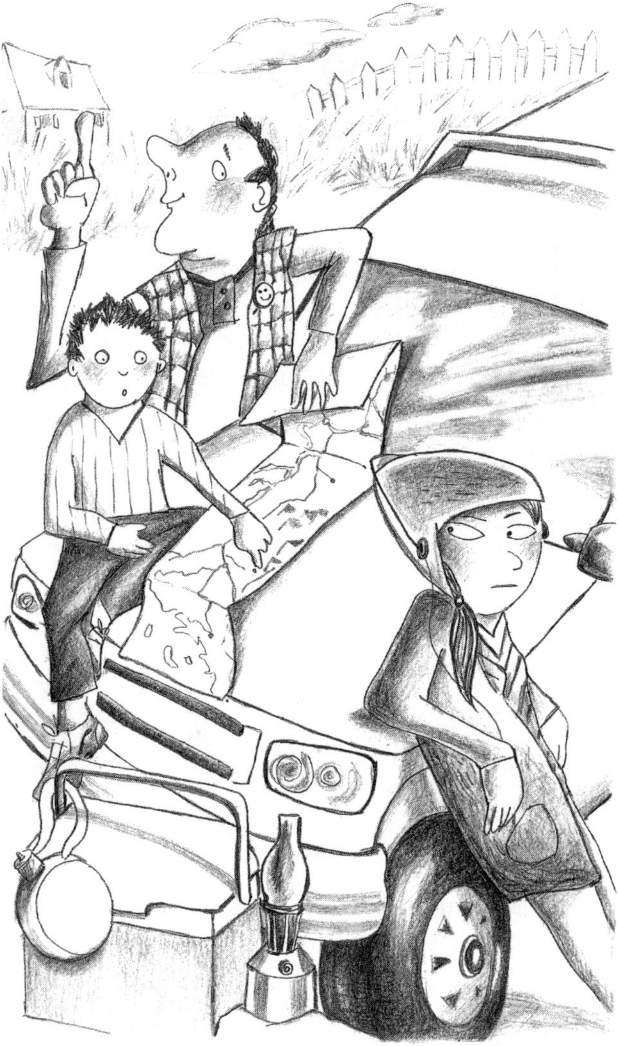

1. Family Bonding

"That is a great idea, Fred. I cannot wait to tell Jessica and Ben. We will have such fun going camping together."

I was putting a video into the TV as the sound of Mom and Fred talking came through the open door. "Oh, no, not that!" I thought. "That is the last thing I want to do. They will not catch me going on a camping trip with him!"

Fred was our new stepdad. We did not like him much. For one thing, he kept trying to be friends with us. It was as if he thought he could take the place of our real father. He kept talking to us and hanging around all the time, trying to make jokes. He liked to show off and brag about things he had done. I think he was trying to make himself look good to us. But to Ben and me, he seemed like a big fake.

The sad thing was, we were stuck with him. He was in Mom's life, and now he was in ours. But we did not have to like him.

I will say one thing. Since Fred came into the family, I did not fight with Ben so much. Nine-year-old kids can be a pain. At least for now, Ben and I found we had to stick together against Fred.

Mom and Fred were still talking. I moved close to the door.

"I bet Jessica and Ben have been dying to go on a trip in my new four-wheel-drive SUV," said Fred.

I thought to myself, "Is he nuts? We do not want to go anywhere in his SUV!"

Fred went on. "I know this will be just the thing for bonding as a family. We will be way out in the desert. There will be no rock music, just rocks. We will have the mountains, the hot desert sun, and a bright moon at night. Jessie and Ben will love it. There will be no radios, no phones, and no TV. There will just be us, for three days of camping in the desert."

"Bonding?" I thought. "Great outdoors? No phones? No radio? No TV?" I felt sick. This camping trip was going to be like being in jail.

Moving fast, I snuck back over to the TV and turned the sound up some. Then I ran to Ben's room. "Ben! We are doomed! Mom and Fred are dreaming up a camping trip."

Ben was working on the computer. He was on the Internet, downloading cheat codes for his video game. "Uh, huh?" he said in a dreamy way.

I shut his door and flopped on his bed. "I said, Mom and Fred are planning to take us out to the desert."

"What, and leave us there?" asked Ben.

"No, but it might as well be. It is their idea of a fun family trip. Fred wants to show off again, this time with his SUV. They were talking about no phones, no music, no TV, no video games."

"I am not going on that trip," said Ben.

"How can we get out of it?" I was racking my brain for ideas.

"Jessica! Ben!" Mom yelled.

"Drat! Here it comes," I said. I felt like an animal in a trap. I sprang up from the bed, opened the door a crack, and yelled back, "In here, Mom!"

Fred and Mom were at the door. Mom led off with, "We have some fun news, you two."

Fred made a sound with his throat. "We're going camping, kids . . . next weekend, out to Stovepipe Springs, in the desert. My new SUV is just the thing for a family trip. And I must say, I am about the best off-road driver I know of."

"When will he stop bragging?" I thought. "Mom—how could you!"

I looked at Mom, trying to show her that this did not sound like fun to me. But she did not get it. She was all smiles.

"I will see about getting a day off from work, so we can all go together," she said. "It will be a great new experience for us. Fred will teach us everything he knows about camping." Mom was babbling on, trying to get us to like the idea. She looked at Fred, then at us. "He knows quite a bit, you know."

Fred looked at me. "And who knows, Jessica. We will be off-road. Maybe I will let you drive the SUV part of the way. I could teach you something about driving. After all, next year you will be old enough to take your driver's test."

Mom gave Fred a look and a little kick. I could tell she did not want him to let me drive off-road, just so he could get on my good side.

I squeezed my eyes shut. I wished I were on a planet millions and millions of miles away.

Ben was the first to answer. "I am not going," he said, without looking away from the computer screen.

"I do not want to go on a camping trip in the desert, Mom!" I said.

Mom and Fred did not say anything. Mom's lips went from a friendly smile to a thin, pressed line above her chin.

"Young man, you will be going on this trip," Mom said to Ben. "And so will you, Jessica, so do not think about ways to stay home. This is a time for all of us to have some time together."

I could feel the trap closing. But maybe there was still a chance. "Aw, Mom," I whined, "please let me stay home. I hate camping."

"How do you know you hate camping when you have not been camping?" chimed in Fred.

My last-ditch words were, "What about Bonnie, Mom? Can she come with us? Please do not make me go without Bonnie!" Bonnie was my best friend.

"Jessica Rae, please stop talking back this way. This trip is for us. It is not for anyone else. We are going camping and that is that!"

I could tell I was walking on thin ice, so I backed off. I ran into my room, closed the door, and sank down next to my bed. My life was over!

2. Madman on the Road

The week dragged on. Every day the sinking feeling in my gut got deeper. I tried over and over to get out of it. But in the end, Mom had the last say. Ben and I had to go.

Then, just a day before the trip, another bad thing happened. Our mother got called away on a sudden company trip. She had to go to a trade show for five days, because one of her bosses could not go.

You would think that she would call off the camping trip. You would think that she would save us from going with Fred. But no. All Mom said was, "I wish I could go with you, but do not stop the plans for the camping trip. It will still be a good experience for you all. You three will have a chance to get closer as a family. You can tell me all about it after I get back."

Now Ben and I were stuck with Fred. Because Ben was so young, he was not much help with getting all the camping stuff together. So that job fell to me, meaning I had to work with Fred on it.

On the day of the camping trip, we had all the stuff lined up on the driveway. Everything was all set to be put in the back of the SUV. Fred was strutting around. He was bragging about his vast camping experience again. He had one tale after another about the desert or the mountains. I just wished he would stop talking. I put my headphones on under the hood of my sweat top.

We loaded up the camp stove, dishes, and food. We had pots for cooking and washing. We had sleeping bags, pads, a tent, a hatchet, paper, and matches. We had jugs of water and flashlights. We had more than enough batteries. We had sunscreen, hats, and sunglasses. We even had a first aid box and a snakebite kit. Snakebite! I could go my whole life without seeing a snake and be very happy about it.

Fred told us we would need thick jackets. I had a hard time believing this. We were going out into the hot desert, right? I did not think we would need those jackets, but Fred made us bring them.

At last Fred gave up on talking to me. Instead he made a big deal over showing Ben the maps. I leaned on the side of the SUV and looked the other way. But I turned down the sound on my CD, so I could hear what Fred was saying to Ben.

Fred's maps were made just for people who were going off-road. The maps showed all the trails, roads, and camping places. He showed Ben where we were headed. The map showed the shapes of the mountains and dry gulches. It showed where lakes and streams were. Fred said that most of the lakes and streams would be dry at this time of year, unless it rained. He talked to Ben about how to read the map. He was saying that you could tell where the land was steep by looking for lines that were close together on the map.

"Jessica, you might want to take a look at these maps, you know," Fred called over to me. I kept looking the other way. I did not want Fred to know that I could hear him.

At last, we got on the road. Ben sat up front with Fred. I claimed the backseat. Ben was getting into the map thing. He was following the roads we were driving on. Then Fred turned up the music on the radio. He began to sing at the top of his lungs. He drove fast and took the turns real fast. I bet he thought it was funny to slam me this way and that in the backseat. I was thinking, "Good thing for seat belts."

After a while, we were miles and miles away from the city. We turned off the main highway.

We set off on roads made of gravel and dust. The land was rocky and flat. For miles, the only plant life we could see was cactus and low brush. The roads were full of ruts and gullies. The air was really hot.

Fred liked bumping the SUV through ditches and over small bushes. From time to time, he would go off the road, just for fun. I began to think we were in the hands of a madman. And this madman wanted to teach me how to drive?

Then the road got steeper, with more turns. We were headed up into the mountains. It was very hot and dry. Fred put down his window and yelled out, "Hooooo-eeeee! Is this fun, or what?" He pulled the wheel of the SUV to the left, grinding the truck suddenly into a sandy streambed. "Why not go this way? This four-wheel-drive SUV can take anything! I will show you!"

I hid my face in my sleeve. This did not look good to me. What if he ran over a cactus? Those spines could punch into rubber and give us a flat. What would we do then?

Fred revved the SUV, racing through the streambed. I hung on tight to the handgrip over the door. The wheels spun in the sand, then grabbed. That was close! I may not know much about the desert, but it seemed to me we almost got stuck.

"Fred, what happens if we get stuck in the sand?" I yelled over the sound of the car.

"Stuck? We will not get stuck!" Fred yelled back. "Not with me driving!"

Just then, Ben said, "Look out, Fred, there is a big rock in the way!"

Fred yanked on the wheel and turned the SUV just in time to miss the rock. Then the wheels hit some more sand. This time we did not keep moving. We were stuck. Fred revved on the gas, spinning the wheels madly, but the SUV still did not go.

I looked back the way we had come. I was surprised to see how high up we were. The gully in back of us stretched downhill into the bright sun. The flat part of the desert was way out in back of us.

I felt a cramp in my gut. Talk about a bad dream coming true! Now we were stuck in the sand, miles and miles from home.

"That is about as far as we will go for now," said Fred. "I think we will turn around here."

"He is nuts!" I thought. "There is no room to turn around." Fred tried to back up the truck, but the wheels still spun. I could not wait to see what he would do next.

Fred jumped out of the truck, ran to the back, and got a spade out. He dug some sand away from the wheels. Then he pulled the floor mats out of the SUV and laid them behind the wheels.

"Hang on, kids," he said. He hopped back behind the wheel and stepped on the gas. He made the truck rock a bit, and the wheels spun again. Then they grabbed on the mats. We were moving again, slowly. Fred backed the SUV a way down the gully. When we got out of the sandy part, he stopped the car. Then he walked back to pick up the mats and the spade.

When he got back to the SUV, he was smiling.

"You see, that was no problem for old Fred. Are we having fun yet, you two?"

I was wishing I could be on the other side of the world. I gave thanks inside that we were at least headed back to the road.

We kept going up, up, and up into the mountains. The road turned this way and that. Soon we were driving along a steep cliff. The SUV was hugging the side of the mountain. On one side of the truck, the cliff went way up, out of sight. On the other side, the cliff dropped off out of sight.

The sun had dropped low in the sky. It was late in the afternoon. I thought, "Where are we going to set up camp? It is getting late!"

Then Ben spoke up. "Say, Fred, will we be stopping soon to set up camp?"

"You got it, Ben. I think we will be there soon," answered Fred.

As if to prove we were almost there, Fred stepped on the gas hard. The SUV sped up fast, just at a place where the road turned hard to the right. Then it happened. Fred grabbed for the wheel, just as we hit a big rock in the road. His hand slipped on the wheel. He grabbed for it again and pulled. Too late! He missed the turn.

Fred slammed on the brakes. The car slid on a million small rocks. Everything seemed to slow down. It was like we were in a dream. We were headed for the cliff! One wheel slid off the road. Still the SUV did not stop skidding. We were going over the side!

I remember screaming as the SUV flipped over. Ben was screaming, too. Then everything went blank.

3. The Long Night

I do not know how much time passed. I just remember part of what happened. The next thing I knew, I was hanging upside down, inside the SUV. Puffs of dust were still hanging in the air. I do not think I had blacked out for long. I was hanging by my seat belt.

It was hard to tell how far the car had slid downhill. I know we flipped at least one time. I looked out the open window next to me. I could see some blue sky, some bushes, and the steep bank of the hill going up. The roof of the SUV was smashed in. It was less than an inch from my head. It was smashed in more where Fred and Ben were. They were hanging from their seat belts, too. It looked like the hood of the SUV had smashed into a rock.

We had been thrown around when the SUV turned over. More than one place on my arms and legs had been bumped. My right arm was throbbing.

Ben and Fred were still, but I could hear them breathing. "Ben?" I croaked. My throat did not want to work, from the dust and the shock. "Ben? . . . Fred?"

"Jessie, are you OK?" Ben sounded all right. At least he was talking.

"I think I am OK. How about you?"

"I am OK. I have broken glass all over me. The front window is smashed."

"I see it, Ben. Can you move?"

"I am still in my seat belt, but I have room to move. I got bumped a bit. I think . . . I think I am OK." He sounded very shaky.

I had to keep my cool. Ben was just a little kid. "I am glad you are OK, little bro."

Fred gave a deep groan. "Fred? Are you OK? Fred?" I asked.

Fred groaned again but did not answer.

"I do not think he is doing so well, Ben," I said. "The car is smashed in on him. Can you see if his legs are free? I do not know if he can move."

Suddenly I thought of what might happen next. "Ben, we have to get out of here! What if the gas is leaking? What if the car explodes?"

I sniffed the air. It did not smell like gas. That was a good thing. "Just a sec, Ben. I do not smell gas, but I still think we should get out fast. I am going to try and get out this window."

Ben said, "I think I can get free of the seat belt and get to the backseat, Jessie. Then I can follow you out the window."

Ben and I worked ourselves free of the smashed SUV. We moved away from the crash site as best we could. The SUV was resting on a flat place in the cliff about 20 feet under the edge of the road. In fact, the cliff was not all that steep right at this part. We could easily make our way back up to the road.

The back end of the SUV looked OK. But the hood and driver's window were all smashed in. Ben and I sat on some rocks to get our thoughts together.

What now? We were miles out. We had not seen one car other than ours. Night was coming on. Fred might be trapped inside the SUV. We might have to set up camp for the night. What should we do first?

Another groan came from inside the SUV. Ben and I crept up to the car. Fred was waking up and trying to talk. We went to the back window and peeked inside. We could see Fred's head and chest, but that was all.

"Fred, can you move?" I asked. "Can you get out?"

I could tell he was in pain because for once he was not talking and joking. He sighed, trying to speak. "I . . . I . . . I cannot move. My . . . leg . . . trapped . . . pain! May . . . be . . . broken. . . ." It was hard for him to talk.

I thought of something. What if Fred's leg was bleeding? "Fred, do you know if your leg is bleeding?"

"I cannot . . . tell," he gasped weakly. "Can . . . you . . . see?"

"Ben," I said, "I think you need to go back in there and see if Fred is bleeding. You are not as big as I am. If he is bleeding, we will have to try and stop it. I will see if I can fish some things out of the back."

I pulled out the tent, sleeping bags, food, water, flashlights, and our backpacks. I thought it might be a good idea to get a blanket or sleeping bag around Fred. The air was still hot. But if Fred was in shock, he might need to be kept under a blanket.

"How is it going in there, Ben?"

"I do not see any bleeding, Jessie. I see part of his leg. It is bent funny. It may be broken."

I was glad there was no bleeding. I was not trained in first aid. I stuffed Fred's sleeping bag through the window of the car. "Ben, see if you can spread this over him. He will need it. Then come on out. We have to look for a spot to set up camp."

"What about some water or food for Fred, Jessie?" asked Ben. "I do not know if he can eat. Maybe we should see if he wants some water."

I passed a jug of water into the SUV. Ben pushed off the cap and spilled some water inside Fred's lips. "Thanks . . ." Fred gasped.

Ben and I went about setting up our camp. We did not want to be too close to the flipped SUV, or too far from it. We did not want to get far away from Fred, in case he needed us. On the other hand, we did not want to miss a car that might come by on the road. The SUV could not be seen from the road. So, Ben and I went up to the road. We dragged some rocks and logs into the road. We made a kind of roadblock. If any cars drove by, they would have to stop. One of us would stay up and watch for cars. We did not have much hope that any cars would come by, but it might happen.

We picked a flat place to camp, off to the side of the crash. Setting up camp was not easy. We did not know how the tent worked. In the end, we gave up on the tent. We got out our sleeping bags. We would just sleep in them and forget about the tent.

Then the sun went down. I could not believe how cold it got. I put on my long pants and sweat top. I put on my jacket, too. It was a good thing Fred made us bring those jackets!

We grabbed two flashlights from our pile of things and flipped them on. They shone brightly.

"Where are the batteries, Jessie?" said Ben. "I want to keep them close by in case one of the flashlights goes out."

We had to poke around a while before we found the flashlight batteries. Then we needed to eat. A strong wind had come up. The desert brush was dry. We thought it would not be wise to get flames going out there. So we made do with eating cold food. We opened up a box of crackers and found a knife for cutting into a brick of cheese. There were some plums and peaches, too. We each opened a can of pop and drank it. We had plenty of snack foods—that was one good thing. The food was good and helped some.

As the daylight dimmed, we saw some things with wings flying around. I think they were bats! We planned to take turns sleeping and staying awake. We would need to check on Fred at least once an hour. We would give him water and try to get him to eat. But he was in great pain and did not feel much like eating.

By then it was really dark. The moon was not up yet. Suddenly an animal called out in a high-pitched "Yip, yip, yip! Yip, youuuuuuu!" It was close by. Ben and I looked at each other. It sounded like some kind of dog. It was not that far from us. Maybe it was chasing a jackrabbit. We sank deep into our sleeping bags and hoped it did not feel like chasing us.

We spent a long night trying to keep out the cold and hoping for no trouble from animals. I admit, we did not sleep much. We took turns checking on Fred and our roadblock. Fred was cold too, and still in pain. Like us, he had trouble sleeping.

Huddled into our sleeping bags, Ben and I talked over what to do next. Should we wait for help? Chances were slim that others would come by. Should we try to walk out and get help? If so, which way should we go? We had just come over a whole mountain. Should the two of us go for help, or should one of us stay with Fred? What would happen to Fred? Were we doomed to die out here in the desert? A million questions without answers raced through my head.

4. Our Plan

The sun came up at last. The wind died down. The sky was gold and pink and very, very big. All night, I had thought of nothing but what to do when daylight came.

When the sun came up, Ben and I had a bite to eat. Some hot drinks or hot food would have been good. We still did not feel like fooling with the stove. I could just see the papers: "Family Crashes, Then Dies in Desert Blaze." No way did I want to mess with flames. So we had cold food again.

Ben said, "Jessie, we cannot just stay here and wait. We have to go look for someone who can help us." It was true. One of us would have to go for help. I thought it should be me.

"Ben, I wish we could walk out of here together, but I think we have to split up. I think I will need to go. You stay here with Fred. You will need to keep watch on the road, too, in case someone comes by."

Ben did not say anything. I could tell he did not want to stay here alone, but he did not fight me.

"The problem is, I do not know where we are. I just know it is a long way out from here."

"What about Fred's maps, Jessie?"

Fred's maps! Why did I not think of the maps? "Do you know where the maps are, Ben?"

"I think they are next to the driver's seat," said Ben. "I will try to find them." Ben grabbed a flashlight and trotted over to the SUV.

He looked inside and said a word to Fred. Fred did not answer. "Jessie," Ben called softly to me, "I think Fred is sleeping!"

"Try not to wake him then!" I answered back.

Ben slipped in through the side window. He was getting fast at this move. I stooped outside the window so I could see in.

"Can you see the maps?"

"Shhh," said Ben. "I'm looking for them."

Ben poked around the seat where Fred was pinned. He found a road map and some backcountry maps and passed them out to me. Then he eased himself out of the car.

Even with the maps, it was hard to tell where we were. We opened the road map. We traced along the highway from the city where we live. Looking over the map, we could see the desert and mountain area. An "X" was on the map. Maybe this was where Fred was headed for our camp-out.

We looked at the off-road maps. One by one, we saw how they fit together. We spread them all out on a flat rock. We used rocks to hold them down so we could study them.

After studying them a while, we began to make sense of them. We could tell where the roads and trails were on the maps. We could also tell where the mountains and streams were. We thought we found the part with the switchbacks where we got stuck. We looked around at the landscape. Then we turned the maps around and lined them up with the sun in the east and the peaks we could see. We thought we could tell about where we were.

As far as we could tell, we were about 40 miles away from a road stop called Ghost Ranch Outpost. I remembered passing it. It was little more than a gas and food stop. "They must have a phone there," I said to Ben. "But there is no way I can walk 40 miles in one day. The road goes way up and over and around this whole mountain. It is way too far to walk back."

We looked at the maps some more. "Ben, do you see this part? It looks like a long dip between the mountains. This line is a stream, right? It must be down below us somewhere. A stream goes down through the dip, all the way to Ghost

Ranch Outpost. If I keep walking down the road, it will cross the stream. Then I can take the streambed down to the Outpost.

"Plus, it will not be as far . . . only about, what, 15 miles, maybe? If I follow the stream, I will not have to go back up all the switchbacks and over the whole mountain."

"Jessie, how are you going to go down that gully? There could be all kinds of animals there. What if you cannot get through? What if something happens to you? What if it rains and the gully fills up with water? What if you step on a snake? What if . . ." Ben was crying then. "How will I know if you run into trouble?" he asked, wiping his eyes and looking up at me.

"It is a big risk, Ben. But backtracking by road is a big risk, too. It is too far by the road. I will find a way to get through the streambed. We need to get help for Fred, fast. I think I can make it down that streambed on my own." I was not 100% OK with doing this by myself, but it sounded good.

"And it is going to be very hot when the sun gets higher. If I follow the stream, maybe it will have water in some places. These little dots on the map . . . they are springs, right? Springs will have water in them, right?" Now I was trying to make it sound good to myself.

"Jessie, all the streams are dry, you know that! Fred was driving in the streambed way down there, remember? It was dry as a bone. You have to take water with you!"

"Yes, and I have to leave enough here for you and Fred, too. I will take water and food and this map. Meanwhile, if someone comes by road, then you know where I will be. I will be somewhere along that streambed."

Ben and I went up on the roadway. We dragged more dry branches out into the road. One of Fred's jackets was set up as a flag. We used my lipstick to write the word "HELP" on the flag. Ben would keep watch on the road, but sometimes he would need to be away to get food or help Fred. If anyone came by, they would at least see the flag.

"Ben, you will need to watch Fred closely. We have to help him. Try to get him to eat something. Get him to drink water. Stay close to him."

I got set to go. It was going to be hot, but I kept on my long pants. Going overland in the desert would mean going through some thick brush. Besides, I did not want my legs ripped up by cactus spines. I put on my hat and sunglasses. I put on plenty of sunblock. Then I stuffed my sweat top and jacket into my backpack. I also packed a flashlight and a pack of batteries. I was not planning on spending another night outside. But that was only if things went well and I reached Ghost Ranch Outpost before nightfall!

I packed two jugs of water. I hoped that would be enough water for the day. Some big chunks of cheese and a handful of crackers went into the backpack. So did a small bag of nuts and one of plums and peaches. I packed a pocket blade and a small camp hatchet. I hated to think about snakes, but I got the snakebite kit out of the first aid box. That seemed to be a good idea, just in case. I put the kit in my backpack. Two of the maps went in my jeans pocket. I would need the maps.

I was all set. No sense in waiting—I had a long way to go. I gave Ben a hug and slung on my backpack. I set off down the road. Then I turned and waved good-bye. "See you later, Ben . . . soon!"

Ben waved and gave a thin smile. "Bye, Jessie! Good luck!"

I looked out over the side of the drop-off, down the steep hill. The streambed was somewhere down there, out of sight. I would have to find it.

5. Ben and Fred

> That day turned out to be the hardest day of my life. But back at the camp, Ben was faced with troubles of his own. Here is his story:

Ben watched Jessie walk away. He felt like yelling out, "Do not go, Jessie. Do not leave me here." What if she got lost? What if she did not reach help? But he kept still. It would not do any good to cry out.

Ben got a jug of water. He looked for some food that he thought Fred could eat. Then he walked down to the smashed SUV. He slid inside to check on Fred. "Fred?"

Fred was waking up. "Ben? Is that you, Ben?"

"Yes . . . I have some water and something to eat here. Do you want some?"

Fred just nodded. Ben helped get some water into Fred. Then he helped him eat a few bites.

After he had some food, Fred began to talk. "Thanks, bud. . . . I am not much good right now. I am hanging upside down, pinned inside my car. My leg is in really bad pain. The pain will not go away. I am really stuck."

"It is OK, Fred. Jessie says we will be OK."

"Where is Jessica?" Fred asked.

"She left a little while back. She went to find help."

It was hard for Fred to talk. He seemed not to get it. "What? Where is she? Where did she go?"

"She walked down the road to find the streambed. She is going to try and get to Ghost Ranch Outpost. They may have a phone there."

"I see," said Fred weakly. "I made . . . that turn. . . . I was going too fast. Now . . . I'm sorry, bud . . ." Fred stopped talking. The talking made him sleepy.

Fred tried to push himself over in the seat. He tried to move. It was no good. He was trying to talk again. "Ben . . . car phone . . ."

"What?" Ben did not think he was hearing right. Was Fred talking about a car phone? Ben did not know Fred had a car phone.

"Ben . . . phone . . . under the seat . . . somewhere here."

Ben could not believe it. Fred had a phone in the car? They could call for help. He and Jessie had not thought about a phone.

Fred could not talk any more. Ben began to look around in the SUV. He slid his hand under the seat, which was now overhead. Nothing there.

"Fred . . . I am looking under the seat for the phone. I cannot find it," Ben said.

Fred did not answer. He was too wiped out.

Ben looked around the side and roof areas of the SUV. He poked his hands around things. He said, "If I can find the phone, maybe we can call for help."

He felt around the seat and the door. His hand swept across something that moved. It was the phone! The door was partly crushed in, so the phone was trapped there. No good. He could not reach it.

6. The Streambed

I had one thing going for me. It was downhill all the way. This would help me make good time. I tramped one way, then the other, down the switchbacks on the road.

The sun kept rising until it was quite high in the sky. Not a wisp of a breeze moved the air. It was just plain hot and dry. Light beads of sweat broke out on my upper lip. I stopped to wipe my face. I pulled out my water and drank a few gulps.

The road was not going down any more. I was at the low part of the mountain, at the end of the switchbacks. It was time to look for the streambed. I did not think it would have any water in it. How could I find a dry stream? What does a dry stream look like, anyway? I thought about the day before. Fred drove through a streambed. I remembered thick brush and the sides of the gully made by the stream. I remembered the sand and rocks. That was it! I would look for a low place with sand and rocks.

I scanned the road and the sides of the road for the place where the stream would cross it. I came to a low part of the road. It was streaked with sand and spotted with a few rocks. There! Yes, water had flowed across the road here. Thick green shrubs and some large trees grew along the path of the stream on each side of the road. "That makes sense," I thought. "It is dry right now. But the streambed would have more water than other areas. So there would be more green plants here."

I stopped and got out the map. I studied the area where I thought I was. Yes, I had the right place, just after the end of the switchbacks.

I turned off the road and into the streambed. A small chill went up my spine. From now on, I could not be seen by anyone on the road. "Why have no other cars come by?" I thought. "Not one! It must be such a bad area that no one likes to camp here! No one but Fred!"

Maybe it was not a nice thought. I felt bad about Fred having a broken leg and a smashed SUV. But I still blamed Fred for bringing us out here in the first place.

The plant life was thick. At places it was hard to get through it. I pushed branches away as I walked. I tried to step lightly on the rocks that filled the bed of the stream. I kept working my way downstream.

I was glad I had my hat on. It kept the sun off the top of my head. But I could still feel the heat of the sun on my neck.

I kept going down the dry creek. I kept hoping to see some water in the stream. But it was dry, dry, dry. The stream had cut deep gullies with steep banks on the sides. It was easy to see that water sometimes moved fast through here. How else could those big rocks and twisted tree stumps have gotten into the streambed?

I followed the creek around a bend. All of a sudden, I stopped. What was this? It looked like the stream split off into two parts. I did not remember this on the map.

I yanked the map out of my jeans pocket. I studied the path of the stream on the map. Yes, there was the road. Here was where I was heading downhill. I traced the line of the stream all the way down to the flatlands. I was not in the flat desert yet. The map did not show any other stream.

I sat down on a big rock to think a bit. Which one was the right stream to follow? I had no time to get lost! I had to get to Ghost Ranch Outpost. I did not have time to make a mistake. Which way should I go?

I looked as far down each stream as I could. "Maybe they came back together somewhere downstream," I thought. "In any case, I am not getting anywhere as long as I am stopped here. I may as well just pick one or the other."

I looked each way, one last time. Then I headed down the left-hand branch of the creek bed. I kept going for while. The streambed was getting small. It was getting very hard to follow. I began to think that maybe I had made a mistake. Then, all traces of it just seemed to dry up.

I looked around. I could not keep going this way. There was nothing to follow. Rats! I should have chosen the other path. Now I would have to find my way back to the top of this branch of the stream.

I hoped I could find the way. Only small traces gave a clue as to where the streambed lay. I was losing time! And now I had to make my way upstream. I glanced at the sun. This little side trip would cost me over an hour of the day's priceless time.

Rushing as best I could, I hiked uphill, picking my way through the cactus and brush. At last I began to see more of the type of plants that grew in the streambed. With each step, the traces of the stream grew more and more easy to follow. After a bit, the gully was easy to see.

By the time I came to the branching-off place, the sun was high overhead. I still had at least ten miles to go. I hoped I could get to Ghost Ranch Outpost before night fell. I thought about how cold it got when the sun went down. I did not want to spend another night in the desert.

A low shrub gave a small patch of shade. I sat down in the shade and drank some water. I got out some food and had a snack. It felt good to be out of the sun, even for a little time.

Then, to make up the lost hour, I began to run. This made it hard to stay out of the way of the dry branches and cactus plants. Long jeans were hot, but I was glad to have something over my legs.

It seemed like those desert plants had it in for me. One time, I passed close to a clump of cactus that had a lot of tiny spines all over it. My leg brushed the cactus plant just a bit. A clump of spines grabbed on to my pant leg.

Then, before I could think, I used my hand to try and brush the clump off my leg. Pain! I got about a million small cactus spines in my hand. I tried to brush them off. They just stuck in other parts of my clothes and hands. What a mess. The heat and the cactus spines were about to drive me mad.

I sucked in a deep breath and blew it out. No use getting upset and wasting more time that way. Then I remembered my pocket blade. It had tweezers in it.

Those little spines gave me a lot of trouble. I pulled them out the best I could, one or two at a time. Then, keeping the spines away from my hands and clothes, I scraped them off onto a rock. I hoped I had gotten them all.

I was mad at myself for wasting this much time. I was hot and I felt weak. I drank some more water. I could see I was getting low on water. Could I could make it through the afternoon on what I had left? If I ran out of water, what would I do?

I remembered something about people getting water from cactus plants. Up until now, I had thought that whole thing was a joke from cartoons—people cutting into a cactus to get water! What kind of cactus plants had water in them, anyway? But now, I would not be surprised if I had to try that.

I was getting cranky and sleepy. I almost cried. I did not want to be there. I hated the desert. I hated cactus and cactus spines and creek beds and dusty roads and camping. I hated it all! If I got out of this, I would not go camping or hiking again as long as I lived!

7. Snake!

It must have been some time after noon. I was on a steep part of the bank. I was looking down, taking one step at a time through the rocks. All of a sudden, I could hear a soft sliding sound close by. Then I saw something move. A large snake slid across my path. It was not three feet away from me. Surprised, I froze in my tracks! I held my breath in sudden fright. What could I do? Would the snake try to bite me?

All I could think of was RUN! I backed up quickly and turned to run back the way I had come. I just hoped that snake would not follow me. In my haste to get away from the snake, I stepped sideways on a loose rock. I was too close to the small cliff made by the gully. I fell, twisting my leg. I slid on the bank. I was falling! I grabbed at rocks with my hands, but could not hold on.

I hit a big rock. This slowed my fall. Then, my heel grabbed on to a small shelf in the bank. I pushed into the slope with my heel, with all my might. This jammed my leg more. I yelled with pain. But that had done it. I had stopped sliding.

40

I could see that I was only partway down the bank of the gully. I eased my other heel onto the shelf, to take the load off my twisted leg. Which way should I go, up or down? The snake was up there. The thick brush was down under me. I looked down the bank. I did not want to go back up where the snake was. But then, who knows, snakes could be anywhere out here!

I studied the brush down the bank. Well, maybe I could get through that thick brush. It looked thinner than it had been up the gully. I began to move down the bank very slowly. Step by step and hand over hand, I picked my way down. I tried not to lean on the leg that had gotten twisted.

I reached the streambed and kept walking downstream. My leg was in pain, making me limp. My jeans and top were full of dust and rips. My legs and hands were scraped and scratched. Some of the cuts were bleeding. I was a bad sight!

When I came to an open spot, I stopped. I hopped up onto a big rock. I wanted to see the area around me. I gazed down toward the flat part of the desert. How much longer would I need to walk? I hoped the map was right.

I had only part of a jug of water left. I used some of it to clean up the cuts and scrapes on my hands and legs. Then I had a drink. Not much water was left in the jug.

I thought this would be a good time to eat lunch. While I was eating, I got out the map and studied it again. It looked like I might have about six or seven more miles to walk.

I looked at the little dots on the map that showed where springs were. If I could find a spring, my water problems would be over. I could fill up my jugs. I hoped the creek on the map was the creek that I was on. If not, I would be way lost. If I was right about the creek, there would be two springs close to it, off to the east a bit.

I squinted at the map and the land around me. The more I studied the land and the map, the more the map made sense. I could see a flat-topped hill in front of me. It was maybe two miles away. I would pass it on the way down. If the map was right, one of the springs should be just on the other side of that hill.

But should I take a chance on leaving the creek bed? What if I could not find the spring? Going away from the creek bed would slow me down, too. Did I have time to risk it? Or should I look for cactus plants to cut into?

I needed water. I needed it bad. How many more miles could I go without water? I had two peaches and two plums left. Well, those things were wet inside. They would give me some water. I saved them. If I did not find water, I might need them to save me.

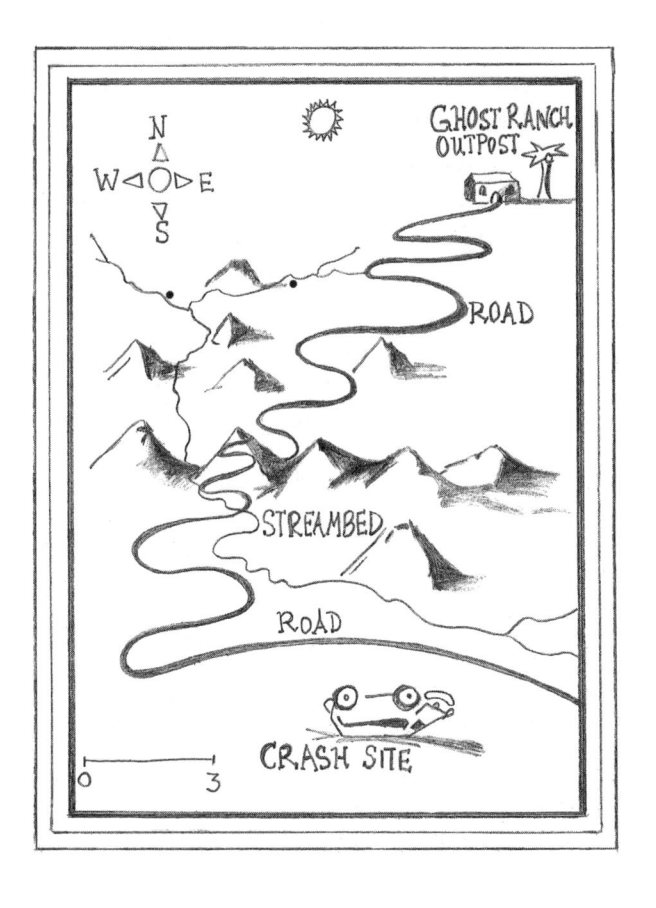

8. The Car Phone

Ben spent hours going between the SUV and the roadblock. He had three things on his mind: Jessie, Fred, and the car phone. He wished he could invent a way to get at that phone. He had tried poking at it from where he could reach. He had tried prying open the door from outside. It was bent and jammed.

After a few hours, Fred woke up again. He ate a little food and drank some water, with Ben's help. Ben could see that Fred felt bad about the crash, too.

"How is your leg, Fred?" Ben asked.

"I must be getting used to it, Ben," answered Fred. He even gave a weak smile. "It feels just as bad, but it seems I can stand it now. I am just tired of hanging around here upside down! Maybe hanging all this time will be good for my brain!"

Ben could not keep from smiling. Fred was back to making jokes, at least for now. He told Fred about trying to get the phone.

"I wish I could get it free," said Ben.

Fred did not say anything. Then he said, "What if we could try sliding this seat? Maybe we can get the seat to move some. Maybe it would make enough space to get the phone free. There is a plastic thing over here under—I mean, over—this side of the seat." Fred moved his head to his right. "It is for moving the seat. If I can push on it, maybe you and I can get the seat to move back. You will need to help. You need to push on the seat when I push on the plastic thing. Try to get the seat to slide."

"Can you reach it, Fred?" asked Ben.

"I am trying . . ." Fred strained to reach up under the seat.

"I am close to it. . . . I . . . There it is! I have it! OK, now! Push!"

Ben pushed on the seat.

"Too late . . . ," Fred gasped. "I could not hold on . . ."

He was sounding wiped out again. But he did not want to stop.

"Try again," said Fred. "One, two, . . . three! Push now!"

He pushed on the plastic, and Ben pushed on the seat. It moved. Just a little bit, but it moved.

"Can you get to the phone now, Ben? See if you can . . . get to the phone!"

Ben worked his hand into the space between the seat and the door. He felt for the phone. There it was. He inched the phone back, a bit at a time. It was so close . . .

Then, it fell free! They had the phone.

"Fred! I got it!"

"That's great, bud. I hope we are in a place where the phone will work. Let me see it."

Fred moved his right hand to grab the phone. He flipped it open with one hand. "Ben . . . here, I have turned the phone on. Now you punch in 911. Wait! Not yet. . . . If you get an answer, you have to tell them where . . . we are."

Fred was having a hard time talking. ". . . 40 miles up road S2 . . . back side . . . Gold Mountain . . . my name . . . you . . . Jessie . . . SUV . . . off the cliff . . ."

Fred had to rest. He sounded weak.

"I will try, Fred," said Ben. He pressed 911 on the number pad. Then he hit "send." He waited. Nothing.

"No ringing," said Ben. "It is not getting through."

". . . Must be . . . too many miles out," Fred said slowly. "Mountain . . . in the way. . . . But you . . . keep . . . trying."

"I will keep trying, Fred," said Ben. "I will try from outside the car. Maybe if I go up on the road." Fred just nodded.

Ben slid out of the SUV. The breeze was picking up. It was starting to blow hard again. Ben looked up at the sky. Off to the east, the sky looked black. All of a sudden, a flash of lightning broke through the black. Ben did not think it was close by. It made a wide and jagged streak in the sky. After a bit, a faint booming sound came through. "Is it raining over there?" thought Ben.

He ran up the bank to the road. He opened the phone and turned it on. He pressed 911 again. Again, he waited.

Again, no ringing. No answer.

Ben felt bad. All that work to get the phone.

The breeze picked up. It tossed the scrubby plants this way and that. Ben looked back up at the sky. Wait! The black part of the sky was growing larger. Was rain on the way?

Ben raced back down to the SUV and slid inside. "Fred! Fred! I saw some lightning out there. It might rain soon!"

At first Fred just looked at Ben.

"Fred!"

"Yes . . . Ben? What is it?"

"I think it might rain. The sky is getting all black. I saw some lightning!"

"Lightning? Rain? . . ." Then Fred seemed to wake up. "Ben! You have to get out of this SUV right now! You have to get to a high place."

"What do you mean?"

"Rain can be a problem in the desert. . . . Water can rush downhill real fast. It can sweep away cars and trees. The water comes fast . . . out of nowhere. It can be many feet high. It does not have to be raining here for a rush of fast water to reach us.

"If that rain is up the mountain . . . you need to get to a high place. This car is in a kind of a ditch. The water can run downhill fast through this ditch. Go! Right now!"

Ben looked at Fred. "But . . . but what about you, Fred? I cannot leave you here."

"You cannot move me. If the water comes through here, you cannot help me. I have to take that chance. But you have to get up high, fast! Now, run! You have to go, Ben!"

Ben did not talk back. He did not want to leave Fred. But he did as Fred said.

Ben went back up to the road and looked around. The sky was black overhead now. The breeze was blowing harder. Up high on the mountain, it looked like it was raining. Ben thought, "Can Fred be right? Can a rush of water really come from nowhere like that?"

Up the road he saw a large rocky ledge. If he could get up onto that ledge, he would be OK.

Then he remembered their things. The food and water. The sleeping bags. The flashlights and batteries. They needed those things. What if he had to spend another night out there?

Ben ran down to the place where he and Jessie had spent the night. He still held the phone in his fist. He dropped it into his jacket pocket. Then, as fast as he could, he stuffed food, drinks, water, and flashlights into his pack. He grabbed the sleeping bags and the pack.

He wanted to get all their things at least up to the road. He tried to hold on to the two bags and run up the bank to the road. It was hard to do. One of the bags slipped out of his hand. He went back to get it.

A few drops of rain splashed on his face. No! Not yet!

He grabbed the bag again and this time made it up to the road. Ben dropped one bag there. He hoped it would not get swept away by water.

All of a sudden, he felt a little funny. There was no fast-moving water. He did not know if he should believe Fred.

He raced over to the rocks and got up as high as he could. He could see the SUV from where he sat. It looked sad there, upside-down. He did not want to think about Fred being trapped inside.

All of a sudden, rain started to fall. Lightning flashed. The dry mountain landscape turned white in the flash. Rain started to fall in great sheets.

Ben zipped on his jacket and sat in the rain. The water began to run in small streams down the road and through the ditch. He kept looking at the water. He could not tell. . . . It might be getting deep in the ditch!

Ben bit his lip. He felt like crying. He was shaking all over, not just from the rain. Fred had been the one to make the car flip over. That was foolish, maybe. But when the rain came, Fred's only thoughts were to save Ben. Ben thought that was very brave. He thought, "Fred just cannot die! He cannot die! It cannot happen that way!"

Ben sat stiffly on the big rock, frozen to the spot. He watched the water flow around the SUV. He did not know how long he sat there in the rain. After a while, the rain began to slow down. At last, it stopped. Little by little, the sun came out.

Ben looked down at the SUV. Water had come through the ditch. Now it was running down the mountain. It was almost all out of the ditch. Ben raced down from the rock and down the bank to the SUV. He slid on the wet mud and sand.

"Fred! Fred!" he yelled. "Fred! Are you OK?"

He looked inside. Fred was not moving. Some water had come into the SUV. The roof was all wet inside. "Fred?"

"I am OK, Ben! The water came in. I got my head scrubbed, for free! But it did not rise very high. The water did not take me or the SUV!"

Ben did not know what to say. He just looked at Fred. His throat choked up. He could not help it. He started to cry. But the crying was from being glad Fred was safe!

9. Get Out of the Way!

The hike was hot, dry, and endless. I was scraped. I was cut. I wanted to be at home and call my best friend, Bonnie. We could have a sleepover and watch videos and play music. I began to think that I would not get to Ghost Ranch Outpost anytime in this life! I began to think I would never hear a CD again or see Bonnie or any of my friends!

Still, I kept pushing one foot after the other. I set the spring as my goal—I needed to get water. I tried jogging again. This time I looked closely at each step. I could not risk another slip. I still had to limp. But I pushed myself so I could make it to Ghost Ranch by sunset.

I was almost past the flat-topped hill. I hoped I could find the spring that was on the other side of it. I came to a place where a small creek bed met the big gully I was hiking down. I thought this was it. "This must be the runoff channel from the spring," I thought. The little channel was dry as a bone. Would the spring have water? Was I being foolish to think I could find a spring in this dry wasteland? I was taking a risk to leave the gully. If anything happened to me, would anyone find me?

The need for water made me go for it. I left the creek bed to find the spring shown on the map. I followed the little creek bed upstream all the way to the base of the flat-topped hill. I kept looking at the map to check where I was. "The spring should be right here!" I thought. I walked all the way to the end of the creek. I did not know if it was the very end. After a while, I could not find any more traces of the creek. I got mad. I do not know why. I had known it was a risk! "The map lied! This map is no good!" I thought in disgust.

"Now I have lost more time!" I wailed to the open desert at the top of my lungs. It did not answer, but I kept on wailing. "And how do I know the map is right about Ghost Ranch!? What if there is no outpost? What then?"

I could have kicked myself. I had lost more time. Should I go look for the other spring? I looked at the map. It was no use. I did not trust the map. "I bet the other spring is dry, too," I thought. "Forget the springs. I will look for a cactus to cut up!" Then I remembered that I still had the plums and peaches.

Now I had to backtrack again. I went as fast as I could back to the big streambed. Suddenly, I could feel a breeze that was quite strong. I looked up at the sky. I was surprised. When did the sky get so black-looking? From the looks of the sky, I thought it might rain. I could not believe it! "In fact," I thought, "it looks like it might be raining back higher up on the mountain. What if it is raining up by Ben and Fred?"

Suddenly, a bolt of lightning blazed across the sky. It lit up the landscape and zigzagged from sky to desert. The lightning strike made dust fly on the desert floor. That lightning was close by! Then it was as if someone had slit open the sky. Sheets of rain began to fall.

This was a happy turn of the road! I almost started dancing! Water at last! I lifted up my face to catch the drops. I opened my water jugs to catch the rain. The openings were too small to catch much. What could I invent to catch the rain?

I looked at the map in my hand. That no-good map! I opened it up and ripped off a part of the map. I kept the rest of the map safe. It was the part that showed the rest of the way to Ghost Ranch Outpost.

I made the map paper into a funnel. I put it so that it would drain into the top of one of the water jugs. That would work . . . at least until the paper got too wet to hold up. Water began to flow into the jug.

The rain was gushing out of the sky. I was soaked, standing there. Talk about funny! Here I was, dying from lack of water. And now, water was all around me. I was so happy about the rain and the water that I forgot about all my cuts and scrapes.

A little thought kept trying to come through my brain. I almost did not remember it. It was something about rain in the desert. Then I remembered. Flash flood! I was in a gully—in a streambed. I had to get to high ground, and I had to get there fast!

I grabbed my jugs of water and ran. I made it to the top of the bank of the gully. It was still sandy there. I did not think I was high enough yet.

A mass of tall rocks formed a peak high over the gully. It was well away from the low, sandy areas. I kept going until I got up on those rocks.

I got up there, and not a bit too soon. I could not believe how fast the water rushed in down there in the gully! The water rose fast, too. It crashed through the gully. Soon the water filled the whole thing from rim to rim. Rocks, trees, and branches were ripped from the land. They tossed in the water like little matchsticks.

The rain, lightning, and crashing sounds went on and on. I sat there shaking. That was close—

too close. I waited for some time for the water to flow by. At last, the water slowed.

Soon the sky was streaked with blue. The sun was low, and the biggest rainbow in the world formed. I could see the whole thing.

I was lost, mad, and sleepy. But the rainbow stunned me—it was so wide and bright. I had never seen anything like it. I had to stop and gaze at it, just for a while.

At last, I picked up my jugs of water and turned downstream again. I walked up on the bank of the gully. The sun was going to set soon. I had to keep going if I wanted to find Ghost Ranch by night.

I began to think that Ghost Ranch had a good name. It was like a ghost, like a dream. I kept chasing after it, but I could not reach it!

10. Ghost Ranch Outpost

"**I**f the map is right," I thought, "I must be getting close to Ghost Ranch Outpost. I will just die if there is no phone there!"

The sun was going down. Then I got lucky. The gully led to a road. At last! By this time, I really did not know where I was. I just hoped the map was right. I thought this was the road we had taken. I thought Ghost Ranch Outpost must not be too far.

Now I was thinking about Ben and Fred. How did they get by this whole day? The breeze came up again, quite strongly. It would soon be time to put on my jacket.

Just as daylight was fading, I saw a rise of dust on the road. A truck was coming up the road! I was almost too wiped out to raise my hand up to flag down the driver. The driver of the truck stopped right next to me. He opened his window and called out my name.

"Are you Jessica?" he asked.

How did he get my name? How did he know me? At first I was too shocked to speak. "Yes, but who ... how ... ?"

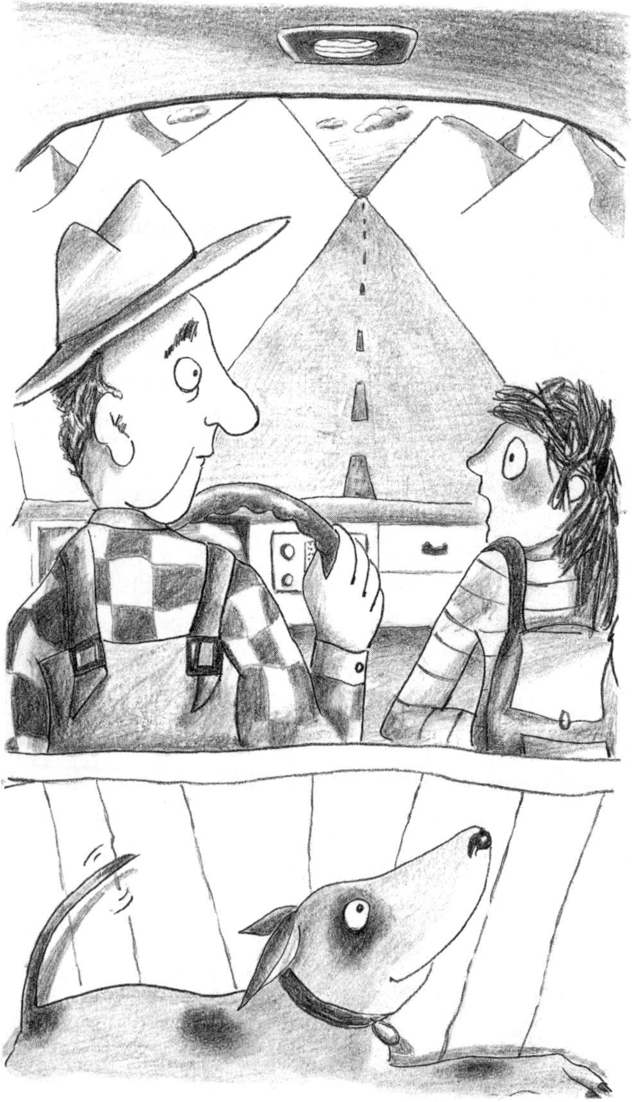

"Let me tell you what has happened, Jessica. I am Al. We got a call from Ben about the crash."

I still did not get it. How in the world did Ben make a call and reach this fellow in a truck?

"Ben!? How did Ben call you?"

"Ben had a car phone."

I did not know there was a phone. Now I really felt bad. I just about lost it. Here I was, tramping through the desert all day. And Fred had a car phone all along! This did not make any sense.

"I did not know Fred had a phone!"

"It has been less than an hour since I talked to Ben," said Al. He spoke in a soft, friendly way. "They had some trouble getting the phone to work. A rescue truck is on its way. It may be at Ghost Ranch Outpost by now. You and I need to get back there fast. Get in!"

I got in his truck. He turned around and gunned the gas. We flew over the bumps and ruts on the way to Ghost Ranch Outpost.

"Are you OK?" said Al, as soon as we got going. It was now getting dark. He turned on the headlights of the truck.

"I have a few cuts and scrapes, but I am OK. I twisted my leg, getting away from a snake."

"Sounds like you had quite a day, young gal!"

"I just want it to be over," I answered.

"Jessica, I did not think I would be seeing you on the road. I thought I might have to hike up the gully to find you. You did a brave thing, coming down that gully."

"I had to leave the streambed a few times," I said. "One time I followed a stream that ended. Another time I was looking for water. I followed the map to a spring, but the spring was dry! I lost a lot of time that way!"

"So many things could have happened to you, Jessica. I am happy we do not have to send a rescue team to find you, too."

I had learned a lot about the desert coming down that gully. "Water rushed into the gully when I was down there," I said. I did not know water could rush in that fast. "I remembered just in time, and got up high."

"You did the right thing."

"Al, did Ben say anything about Fred . . . the driver?"

"Ben said that Fred is OK enough to talk, but he is in a bad way. I think he can hang in there until the rescue truck gets to where you crashed."

"How far is Ghost Ranch Outpost?" I asked.

"It is just up the road, around this bend," answered Al. "Look! The rescue truck is waiting for us."

The red and yellow flashing lights gave the truck away. You could see it from a long way off. Sitting in the truck, I began to feel sleepy. I watched the flashing lights grow close, but I was in a kind of daze.

We turned into the drive of Ghost Ranch Outpost. The team of rescue workers jumped into their truck and drove up to meet us. The driver jumped out and rushed up to Al's truck.

"Jessica? My name is Tom Franklin. We need you to ride with us. Al will stay at Ghost Ranch and wait for your mother. She is on her way here now."

I had not thought about my mother. I was so glad she was coming, I almost cried.

"It is about a two-hour drive to the place where your car crashed," said Tom.

"I hope we can find the place at night, Tom!" I said. "Ben and I put up a roadblock made of tree branches and rocks. You cannot see the SUV from the road."

I got into the right seat of the rescue truck. We waved good-bye to Al and got on the road. The black night was all around us.

Tom said, "We have some tools for cutting and prying open your dad's truck. From the sounds of it, it seems like he is stuck inside the car."

I did not like to hear him call Fred my "dad." But it was a mistake anyone could have made.

"Stepdad," I said. I still blamed Fred for this whole thing. "He . . . Fred . . . went around the bend too fast. The SUV slid off the road and flipped." The whole crash kept playing through my brain like a video. It was a bad dream that kept playing over and over again!

I was afraid that we would miss the place in the dark, or make a wrong turn. I hoped the branches were still blocking the road. I hoped that the rushing water had not swept them away.

The two-hour trip seemed to take more than that at night. After hiking all day, I felt wiped out, but still I could not sleep. I was too full of thoughts of Ben, Fred, and my long hike down from the mountain. I felt I had to keep a lookout on the road. I chewed on my lip and looked out into the black night. This long day was not yet over.

After a while, we started going up. We drove up, up, up, into the mountains. Then we started going down the switchbacks. I remembered them well. We were getting close now.

We came around a bend in the road. A flash of light shone toward the rescue truck. It was Ben! He was waving a flashlight madly. He was standing at the top of the bank. He was next to the roadblock we had made.

Tom screeched the truck to a stop at the side of the road. The rescue team went right to work. They quickly got down to the SUV and used their strong flashlights to light up the area. They looked at Fred and spoke to him.

Tom and his crew got out their cutting and prying tools. They sliced into the SUV and used a crank-type jack to pry back the smashed part.

They made it look easy. They cut Fred right out of the wrecked SUV. Then they put him on a long flat plank. They looked him over while giving him first aid. His leg was broken. He was bashed and cut in some places. But overall, he was OK.

The rescue team had a lot of good words for Ben and me. They kept telling us that we had been very wise not to mess with matches and the stove. They liked the fact that we had not left Fred by himself. And they could not believe that I had walked all that way in the desert heat without getting lost.

For not knowing much about getting along in the desert, we had done great.

At last the rescue team moved Fred up the hill to the road. They whisked him into the back of the rescue truck. Then we were on the way back to Ghost Ranch.

I asked Ben all about what happened while I was hiking. After the rain, Fred had asked Ben to try standing on the rock to use the phone. It was the most open place in the area. It worked. It was the only place where the phone would work. Ben reached 911. Then 911 reached Al at Ghost Ranch Outpost. And Al had reached me.

Then Ben talked about Fred. He kept it low so no one else could hear. He wanted me to know about how brave Fred was when the water was coming. He talked about Fred making jokes, even when he was in pain. It almost sounded like Ben was starting to like Fred.

He said to me, "Fred is not that bad a fellow, and I am glad he is OK."

Well, I did not feel like giving Fred any hugs or prizes. His showing off got us into all this trouble. But I was thankful that we were all OK. And I felt that we had been through a lot, the three of us.

I could see that Ben's head was starting to nod. He leaned his head against me and fell into a deep sleep.

I was glad to be on our way home. I was ready to leave the desert and the mountains. Soon I was sleeping, too, on the way back to Ghost Ranch Outpost.